HOW TO BE PUBLISHED

LYNN MORRISON

Fairlight Books

First published by Fairlight Books 2020

Fairlight Books
Summertown Pavilion, 18–24 Middle Way, Oxford, OX2 7LG

A CIP catalogue record for this book is available from the British Library

ISBN 978-1-912054-56-5

www.fairlightbooks.com

Printed and bound in Great Britain by Clays Ltd.

Cover designed by Amanda Weiss

MIX
Paper from
responsible sources
FSC® C018072
FSC
www.fsc.org

CONTENTS

FOREWORD

There's nothing quite so satisfying as typing the words 'The End' on the last page of the first draft of your book. No matter how long it has taken you to get there, it is a monumental accomplishment. Once the euphoria settles, writers look around and say, 'What next?'

These days, authors have a variety of options for bringing their work to market, ranging from the traditional agent-publisher channel to indie publishers, self-publishing and other alternatives in between. This is great news for individuals who want to have control over their publishing journey, but can be overwhelming to those who are starting out and are unsure which route to market is right for them.

Finding unbiased information to help guide your choice can be challenging. No one publishing method guarantees success or failure. If you speak to other published authors, you'll likely find they champion the path they have chosen for themselves. However, just because it is right for them doesn't mean it is right for you.

Equally, you may feel pressure from family, friends or colleagues to limit yourself to traditional publishing. People who are unfamiliar with today's publishing landscape may be unaware of how well regarded indie, hybrid and self-publishing have become. You could spend years querying a book, hoping for a traditional contract, when other routes might have been similarly valid, and faster.

In researching this book, I went behind the scenes, speaking with a number of authors and publishers to gain an understanding of the pros and cons of each publishing option. These behind-closed-doors, no-holds-barred conversations helped me to identify what evaluation criteria writers should use to guide their decision-making during their publishing journey.

How to Be Published outlines all of the publishing alternatives available to writers today and gives concrete advice on how to select the right one for your book. I would encourage you to keep an open mind and to be honest with yourself as you read through and engage with the quizzes.

If you do so, you will be well on your way to finding the pathway that best suits your book, your personal strengths and your goals for your writing career.

CHAPTER ONE

The Former Publishing Landscape

Twenty years ago, the publishing landscape looked vastly different from today. As an author ready to release a new book into the world, there were relatively few choices for how you might go about it.

In many ways, it was a simpler world. However, formidable gatekeepers controlled exactly who and what was published and decided which books were available to the reading public. Unless you could afford vanity publishing, or were well connected within the literary community, your only options were to secure a literary agent or to send your book directly to one of the few publishers that accepted unsolicited manuscripts. Most books died in either a desk drawer or in the infamous slush pile, where only a tiny proportion made the cut.

Although the number of books published increased in each decade of the twentieth century, particularly once the paperback book format came into existence, the number that made it past the gatekeepers to land on bookshelves was still relatively small in comparison to now.

This original route to market – from writer to agent to publisher – remains remarkably unchanged even today and is still considered to be the 'traditional route' to publication. Its dominance, however, is diminishing as technology opens up new, equally viable pathways for authors to bring their books to market.

Desktop publishing software, digital on-demand printing, online marketplaces and e-readers have caused a fundamental shift in the world of publishing, a shift so profound that some liken it in importance to Gutenberg's invention of the printing press in 1439. Self-publishing became a legitimate path to market between 2000 and 2010, with the total number of books published increasing dramatically in comparison to the previous decade. Suddenly, authors had new ways to put their books in the hands of readers, both through self-publishing and selling via online platforms.

While self-publishing opened the door for thousands of new writers, it also led to an inevitable fall in quality control. Traditional publishers take on the responsibility for editing – including developmental edits, copy-editing and proofreading – as well as cover design, typesetting, production and distribution. Most early self-published authors skipped over these steps, rushing to put their work up for sale without paying for outside support to get their book up to a professional standard. This led to self-publishing gaining negative connotations, both within the industry and with readers.

Thankfully, self-publishing has grown and evolved over the last decade, particularly as successful traditionally published authors have begun making the switch. Cottage industries of independent editors, cover designers, hybrid publishers, writing mentors and book marketing agencies have sprung up to fill the gaps, providing authors with plenty of options for support in the publishing areas that are outside of their core skillset.

Self-published writers have found firm footing in the publishing world by banding together and moving quickly to react to changes in the market. Unlike traditional publishers, many self-published authors view one another as comrades rather than competitors, believing they are better off working together to grow their overall market share. They disclose information, advice and key knowledge to one another, and it is working in their favour. Each year's book sales data shows traditional publishers losing share in a growing market. Self-published authors are now setting the trends, particularly in the digital publishing space where they've perfected the art of co-marketing through newsletter swaps and indie box sets.

Nowadays, it is difficult, if not impossible, to identify a book's publishing path simply by looking at its cover or its place on the sales chart. Traditional publishers, indie presses and self-published authors all compete equally for sales, and the book sales figures reflect this shift.

When you set out to write your first book, it is because you have a story to tell. It isn't uncommon for debut authors to put aside any thoughts of publishing pathways until the first draft of their work is done. Only then, when faced with a completed draft, do many start to think about how best to shape the work and eventually get it into the hands of readers. Before we start to look at which route is best for your book, let's take a look at all of the options, both traditional and newer, in detail.

*

Nowadays, very few publishers accept unsolicited manuscripts. If you want to go down the traditional publishing path, you must first start with finding an agent.

When taking this traditional route, the author sends a sample of their book, usually along with a brief synopsis and a query letter, to a select number of literary agents. The hope is that at least one agent will step forward with an offer of representation. Agents select books either because they fall in love with the writing and decide to champion it, or because they determine it is so marketable that publishers are likely to battle to secure publishing rights – or preferably both!

Most agents these days prefer to receive submissions electronically, either via email or through an online submission portal, but there are still a rare few who prefer a paper submission, requiring a stamped self-addressed envelope for return of the manuscript if rejected.

This process, known as querying, can last anywhere from days to years. Yes, really. Each literary agency approaches the querying process differently, with some replying immediately if they are interested, others guaranteeing a response within a number of weeks, and still more saying broadly that authors will hear back if the agent is interested, with no time frame for when this response might come.

For this reason, it is not uncommon for authors to query dozens or even more than a hundred agents over time, revising their query and manuscript along the way.

I will go into greater detail on the querying process in Chapter Five, including tips on the best way to attract an agent. For our purposes here, the key point to take away is that in the traditional model, the agent acts as a very important gatekeeper when it comes to what reaches publishers. You must get past them to even be considered for publication.

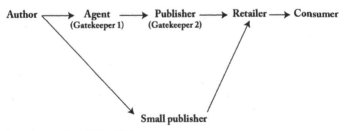

A simple story about BIG publishers
and SMALL publishers

Figure One: The traditional publishing pathway

Once you have managed to secure a contract for representation from a literary agency, the agent will work with you to prepare your manuscript for the next round of submissions: sending it to publishing houses. Writers can be caught unawares by agents' requests for additional rewrites or further editing at this point. Part of the agent's responsibility is to get your work in the best possible shape to make it marketable. They will have their finger on the pulse of the publishing industry, and will advise changes as needed to make your book commercially appealing to publishers. What 'commercially appealing' looks like varies by genre and title, in some cases literally meaning sales potential, in others the likelihood of winning a prize or critical acclaim.

When your agent is happy, they will send the manuscript to a carefully chosen set of editors within certain publishing houses. Agents focus on editors with whom they have a great relationship, who they know are looking for something like your book, or who the agent thinks might fall in love with it and feel as excited about it as they are. For this reason, it is important to choose a literary agent who has experience with your genre and connections within relevant publishing houses.

Now we meet the second set of gatekeepers in the traditional sector: the commissioning editors. These editors will read the book and if they like it and/or think it is marketable, they might make an offer to buy the publication rights, quoting an advanced payment that they would be willing to make to the author.

The 'advance' is a lump sum consisting of a forward payment of royalties that would be due to the author from future sales of the book once it is published. The publisher's offer would usually also clarify the territories (or countries) within which the publishing house would like to have the rights to sell the book.

In the past, such an advance would nearly always have been a significant enough sum to allow the writer to earn a living. Unfortunately, that is less common these days, for a number of reasons that are covered in Chapter Seven. Today's authors are more likely to see either no advance (common when signing with a smaller publisher), a small advance of between £500 and £1500, or a very large advance because there has been interest in the book from a number of different publishers. There is little middle ground.

The big advances, the ones that gain headlines in trade press such as *The Bookseller* or Publishers Marketplace, are extremely rare. This is why they are headline-worthy.

They tend to result from bidding wars between publishers. Bidding wars do not happen by accident. They need a 'hot' book, one which everyone thinks is going to be a big seller, and an agent to handle the tender process so as to maximise the excitement and get those bids going sky high.

Now for the question to which every writer wants to know the answer – what sort of books cause bidding wars? I split them into two broad categories: books by exceptionally famous (or infamous) individuals, and books that appeal to a mass commercial audience. The first category is well out of the reach of most authors, so I will set it aside. The second category requires impressive skill and a modicum of good luck. Not only do you need to have an incredibly well-written and engaging story, you must also find an agent who can convey this to publishers on your behalf. Your agent must convince them that you have produced a book that will appeal to a mass audience, either because of its fresh but still accessible nature or because it is bang on trend.

Trend writing is popular with both traditional and self-published authors, and is known as 'writing to market'. When a breakout book tops the charts, it can pull a number of titles along in its wake. For example, when Catherine Alliott published *The Old-Girl Network* in 1994, she wasn't expecting to create a new genre of fiction. Her tale of modern womanhood inspired bestsellers such as Helen Fielding's *Bridget Jones's Diary* (1996) in the UK and US author Jennifer Weiner's *Good in Bed* (2001), officially creating the chick-lit category of novels, which continued well into the 2010s before losing favour.

A more modern example in crime writing got its start in 2012, when *Gone Girl* by Gillian Flynn topped the bestseller charts, creating a new market for complex female protagonists. Paula Hawkins followed in her footsteps with *The Girl on the Train*, igniting a four-way bidding war over her book, which featured yet another flawed female lead. Authors writing thrillers with a real-life edge to them had an immediate advantage when trying to sell a book into the traditional publishing world.

Writing to market is not limited to fiction. After Adam Kay's big success in 2017 with *This Is Going to Hurt*, which stayed at the top of the Sunday Times bestselling non-fiction charts for a record-breaking fourteen months, agents and commissioning editors were on the hunt for similar works, specifically non-fiction exposé books about people from professional trades, dubbed 'professional confessionals'. Kay's book was quickly followed by the release of more titles in the same genre, including *The Prison Doctor* and *The Secret Barrister*, which each became Sunday Times bestsellers in their own right.

If your aim is to get the biggest advance you can and have your book at the top of booksellers' charts, you must keep a close eye on trends and work quickly to offer agents a manuscript that everyone is currently seeking. Trend writers focus on producing a minimum viable product rather than investing additional time aiming for perfection.

For most writers, writing to market successfully is easier said than done. Unless you are well versed in the trend and are capable of writing quickly, by the time you write the book, the trend may have moved on. You may find yourself offering a psychological thriller manuscript to agents after the psychological thriller market is already swamped with jumping-on-the-bandwagon books.

Writing to market has an additional drawback: it is as much a restriction as it is a guide. The hot trend might not be the book you want to write or may require you to sideline a work in progress.

For many writers, the dream is to set the trend rather than to follow it. Realistically, books like *The Old-Girl Network*, *Gone Girl* and *This Is Going to Hurt* are the exception rather than the rule.

Once you and your agent have agreed to sell the rights to your book to a publisher and once you have signed the contract, you will start working with the commissioning editor on getting the manuscript ready for publication. They may request another round of developmental edits before sending it to be copy-edited, typeset and proofread, getting a cover designed, getting proofs printed for publicity purposes and carrying out marketing activity. In the past, most books would have received some marketing support from the publisher, including the now disappeared 'midlist' books (discussed further in Chapter Seven), but these days, the skewing of advances to a small number of fortunate titles is often reflected in how publishing houses spread their marketing spend.

If a publishing house has paid a large advance for a book, they often feel the need to demonstrate that this was a wise choice. The best way to do so is to make sure the book does what they promised it would do – either topping the charts or winning critical acclaim. They make this happen by allocating a significant portion of their marketing budget to that book.

This is why often you will feel like everyone is suddenly talking about the same book at the same time – the publishing house is spending their marketing budget in order to make sure of this. While it is wonderful if this is your book, for other authors on the list, a lack of marketing support is a common complaint, creating a strong case for the argument: 'If I'm doing the marketing myself, why didn't I just self-publish?' A very valid question!

If you're keen to see your book on the shelves of major brick-and-mortar book retailers, traditional publishing houses hold the strongest relationships with these businesses. The sheer volume of works they publish each year, combined with the long-term nature of the relationship they have with these retailers, gives them a leg-up on everyone else.

*

Within the traditional publishing pathway, there is an alternative to the 'big five' publishers – smaller publishing houses and independent presses. Smaller houses and indie presses usually publish in the traditional way, but they vary in the type of books they publish, as well as in character, scope and expertise.

You don't necessarily need an agent to submit your book to smaller publishers and indie presses, as many of them accept submissions directly. These publishers operate in a similar manner to larger houses, entering into a contract with you to purchase rights to sell your book, professionally editing the book and arranging for a cover. They may also have an in-house marketing team who can support you with your promotional efforts.

When it comes to distribution, some smaller houses have agreements that allow them to access a larger house's distribution network. This does not guarantee that major retailers will stock your book by default, but it does make it easier for your publisher or you to contact them directly to pitch them about stocking your title. For those houses and presses that are not affiliated with a major distribution network, many will have built up their own relationships directly with bookstores which they will leverage when your book is published.

The major benefit of small publishing houses and indie presses is that they usually specialise in a particular genre or subject matter. They may also champion books that mainstream publishers are not interested in publishing, either because the audience for the subject is too small and/ or because the book is just not commercially viable.

You can find examples of great small publishers on both sides of the pond, like Canbury Press (contemporary non-fiction); Arc Publications (poetry); Seren Books (English-language books from Wales); Chronicle Books (children's and adult trade books); Seven Stories Press (human rights and social and economic justice); and of course my publisher Fairlight Books, which started out as a supporter of high-quality literary fiction, a genre that at the time was out of favour with mainstream publishers.

Writers who sell their books to smaller houses and indie presses should be aware that often these publishers are not-for-profit or are even loss-making. This means they generally aren't able to pay an advance and will be limited in their ability to splash your book on billboards or posters at bus stops. However, they are usually passionate advocates of their authors and the books they publish, and can often launch the career of a writer.

As an example, Eimear McBride spent nine years trying to find a publisher for her novel *A Girl Is a Half-formed Thing*, before finally selling it to Galley Beggar Press. Despite a small initial print run of a thousand copies, McBride captivated readers and reviewers alike. Her book won several awards including the Kerry Group Irish Novel of the Year, the Goldsmiths Prize, the Desmond Elliott Prize, the Baileys Women's Prize for Fiction and the Geoffrey Faber Memorial Prize. It was shortlisted for the Dylan Thomas Prize and the Folio Prize, making numerous lists as one of the best books of the year.

In the US, Jesmyn Ward, now a two-time National Book Award winner, found a home for her debut book *Where the Line Bleeds* at Agate Publishing, a small press dedicated to African-American literature. *Essence* magazine selected it for its annual book club, moving it into the spotlight. The book went on to win a Black Caucus of the American Library Association (BCALA) Honor Award and was shortlisted for the Virginia Commonwealth University Cabell First Novelist Award and the Hurston-Wright Legacy Award.

Specialist publishing houses provide the additional benefit of having an excellent understanding of their target readership's demographics. Their immersion within the space, both as publishers and readers, can help you find your niche audience or shape your work so that it hits the mark you were aiming to hit.

My only note of caution here is to do your homework about the publishing house before you sign anything. Contact other authors they have published, ask in forums and writing circles, and search online to see if they are included on websites listing predatory publishers.

Occasionally a company will masquerade as a smaller publishing house, when in reality it is a self-publishing service provider (i.e. they will manufacture a book for you and charge you for the service). The other risk with smaller publishers is their longevity. Check with their authors to make sure they are being paid royalties on time and as agreed. You may also want to ensure your contract gives you the ability to take back your publishing rights in the event they fail to pay, or, worst case scenario, go under.

CHAPTER TWO

The New Publishing Landscape

In 2011, Amazon had 30,000 employees. By 2017, it had 566,000, becoming the twenty-eighth largest company in the world and the fifth largest in the US, with a market cap of $916 billion and annual revenue of $232 billion.

Amazon and other platforms like it have removed the physical barrier between consumers and sellers, creating virtual showrooms for anyone interested in selling, and providing physical warehouses for all of those goods. Shops moved from the high street to our computer screens, and bookstores were as impacted as everyone else.

As you may remember from the introduction, book purchasing wasn't the only thing Amazon revolutionised. In the book market, Amazon is a publisher AND a retailer.

It not only enables readers to buy the books they want, it also helps writers publish their work without the necessity of another intermediary. This innovation has changed how books are sold, as well as which books are sold.

As a result, today's publishing landscape is considerably more complex.

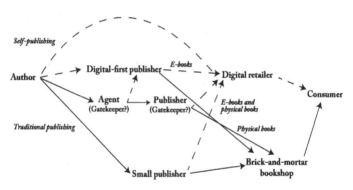

A much more complicated landcape
for a new writer to navigate...

Figure Two: The new publishing methods

Figure Two depicts today's world. Running through the middle of it is the traditional route of agent-publisher-retailer (or indie publisher-retailer) – remaining a strong and vibrant part of the market and responsible for a great number of bestselling books every year.

But now there are a number of other options open to authors which allow them to sidestep the author-agent-publisher gauntlet. On top of indie presses and self-publishing, there are a myriad of hybrids including digital-first publishers and self-publishing service providers.

Writers are no longer stuck with having to pick one path and stay on it. Often authors might start in the self-publishing world and then find an agent approaching them to pull them into the traditional sector, or an author who has long been published by the traditional sector might get frustrated that their books aren't getting the exposure they want and request to have the rights returned to them so they can self-publish instead. Increasingly, authors are taking advantage of this flexibility to have control of their own destiny.

*

Self-publishing is hardly a new concept in the publishing world, despite how much it might seem that way. It has, however, grown in both recognition and market share since technology made wide distribution a possibility for self-publishers.

Self-publishing, in its truest form, means that the author takes on responsibility for every aspect of the publishing process: writing, editing, cover design, production, and marketing and promotion. Someone who self-publishes is, in essence, an independent publisher for a single author – themselves.

Authors interested in self-publishing should not underestimate the work involved. The merry days of publishing a first draft with a homemade cover and hoping for success are far behind us. Readers are highly critical of any book that doesn't uphold accepted quality standards, and they are quick to voice their complaints in the form of online reviews. Professional editing and cover designs are a bare-minimum requirement for any chance at commercial success.

Why do authors choose to self-publish? It offers a number of advantages for individuals willing to put in the effort. Authors retain complete creative control over their work, from making final editorial decisions to choosing the cover art. Authors also keep all of the profits, not having to split them with agents and/or publishers. Profits are paid out more quickly and often with greater frequency. Self-published authors have access to all of their sales data, allowing them to trial various promotional tactics and track their impact.

However, self-publishing is not without risks and isn't viewed the same in every genre. For example, a self-published textbook by an unknown author is unlikely to get picked up by schools and universities. Conversely, self-published books in genres such as romance, mystery, crime, sci-fi and fantasy often perform as well as traditionally published books.

Authors who choose to self-publish must treat their writing as a business. They need upfront investment funds to pay for any professional support – at minimum a professional editor for their early titles – along with production and distribution software. We'll cover the self-publishing process in greater detail in Chapter Six.

*

For many years, the author's dream was to see their book on display in a brick-and-mortar bookstore. Amazon changed all of that. Now many authors choose to launch their work in an e-book format only, testing the waters before investing in printing and distribution. Known as digital-first publishing, this is usually offered either by a smaller publishing house set up specifically as a digital-first publisher, or by a specialist imprint (or brand) of a large publishing house.

What exactly is it? Well, it is what the name suggests. If you sign up with a digital-first publishing house, they will publish your book initially in e-book form only. They are often specialists in promoting e-books and, tying in with this, usually publish those genres that do very well in e-book form – particularly romance, crime and sometimes sci-fi or fantasy. As building a following for the author is very important in genres like these, a typical digital-first contract might be for a three-, six- or even twelve-book deal.

Why would a publisher choose to focus strictly on digital? In addition to lower upfront investment costs and a quicker route to market, digital first provides publishers with more freedom in their pricing strategies. Publishers can work with authors to build a loyal following, offering their first book for free or at a major discount, and gradually increasing book prices as the series takes off. Once the author's books have become commercially viable, they will start to print and distribute paper copies of the books. Hence the term 'digital first'.

Digital-first publishers offer advantages to authors. First, they tend to publish a larger volume of book titles per year. This creates opportunities for debut and emerging authors who are looking to break into the publishing world. Second, the multi-book contracts can provide authors with more of a guarantee of a steady income. Not necessarily a sizeable one, but they won't need to query or work with an agent each time they write a new title.

Authors interested in digital-first publishing should be aware that the speed of getting books to market also impacts on their writing time. Whereas a traditional print publisher might require one new title per year from an author, digital publishers will expect writers to deliver multiple books per year. They will want as many titles as quickly as possible to build up reader loyalty.

Should you choose to publish with a digital-first publisher, you should consider the length of time for which you want to sign away the rights to your works. If the publisher is not successful in launching and promoting your titles, you may want to have the rights revert back to you so that you can self-publish. If you choose an independent or small press, as always, you should do your research into their business before signing a contract.

*

In between traditional publishing and self-publishing sits hybrid publishing. Hybrid publishing is sometimes viewed as a catch-all category for any publisher that shares the publication costs with the author.

What does a hybrid publisher do? Hybrid publishers operate in a similar way to traditional publishers, overseeing the editorial, production and distribution side of the publishing process. What makes them different from other small presses is that they charge the author for these services, and in exchange offer authors a larger portion of the revenue.

Hybrid publishers (many of which specialise in particular genres) that use traditional submission processes to select which titles they choose to publish, and that uphold the highest publishing standards, are often well regarded by the industry and have great reputations. In contrast, vanity presses who will take on anyone willing to pay the cost may not be viewed as favourably, as their titles can fall short of the standards in terms of writing quality, and the usual checks and filters that a traditional publishing house imposes will not apply.

Hybrid publishing is an interesting option for authors who are struggling to find traction in the traditional publishing space or who want to have more control over timelines and the final product, but who do not want to take on the full burden of self-publishing. Hybrid publishers can ensure that your book is of high quality, is well edited and is available through wider distribution networks. They may also provide some marketing support, including submitting titles for prizes and awards.

Non-fiction writers, such as business leaders or memoirists, find hybrid publishing particularly appealing, as their titles face stiff competition through traditional channels where the size of your social media following is often more important than your writing abilities. Hybrid publishers sometimes include writing courses and advisors as part of their package, helping these non-fiction writers create a better book than they could produce entirely on their own.

However, writers should be aware that hybrid publishing still carries risks, and not all publishers are created equal – professionalism varies. Most publishers, of any type, do not make their money back on every individual title. Authors investing in hybrid publishing will be no different. Anyone interested in pursuing this route to market should conduct a detailed review of all the potential publishers, vetting their editorial and design staff. Research their previous titles and speak to as many of their authors as possible to gather information on their experiences. It is far too easy to overpay for publishing assistance if you are unfamiliar with the real cost of editing, layout and cover design.

Writers should be particularly wary of vanity presses who are willing to take on anyone who walks in the door. They are more likely to overcharge for their services, adding little value in the end. You may actually damage your reputation by associating yourself with their list of titles, if the quality of their books is inconsistent or poor.

*

With traditional, independent, digital-first and hybrid publishers as well as self-publishing, authors have a lot more choice about how to bring their book to market. But choice goes side by side with confusion. How do you choose which path to take?

Let's start with a frank conversation about the market for books. One of the impacts of the changes to the publishing landscape is that there are many more books published now than ever before. This isn't simply due to the perceived ease of self-publishing. There has been an explosion in the number of creative writing courses, freelance editors and cover designers. All of this sector growth makes it easier for writers to learn or at least pick up a few of the skills of the craft and to get help with polishing up the final product.

In the publishing model of the past, those gatekeepers – agents and commissioning editors – carefully selected the books that they wanted to release to the marketplace. They had near-total control over the number of books which would be published, as well as which genres and titles. The traditional model aimed to sell a million copies of a few books. The new marketplace and the dominant e-retailer of the sector (Amazon) have a strategy based on selling a few copies of a million books.

The net result of this change is that now a book doesn't have to be well edited, well researched or even well written before it is published. This causes difficulty for all writers as you need to find a way to make your book stand out from an increasingly huge crowd.

All of the traditional publishing rules have changed. The gatekeepers are still opening and closing gates, but the reality is that the walls have been knocked down around them. When it comes to book topics, anything goes. If a reader wants it, the retailing marketplace will provide it. You want your favourite genre in novella form? No problem. You want it in an 800,000-word, six-book box set? No problem. Someone will be there, ready to deliver.

This is why the publishing landscape is a confusing and worrying proposition for new authors. Every path has a pro and a con. If I go down one and it doesn't work out, can I switch to the other? Are some paths better suited to some books than others?

The next chapter offers some answers to these questions. It is definitely the case that some books suit some routes better than others. But it is also the case that some routes suit some *authors* better than others. Whether you want to be a household name, win a literary prize or just have a beautiful book for friends and family to read will make a difference to which path will be best suited to you. Whether you have written an academic work, a blockbuster, a sci-fi epic or a literary masterpiece will all make an impact on which route through the publishing maze is best for you.

If you have a book manuscript completed, these days it is more important than ever to make sure you understand the overall market, your specific genre, and how and where the books in your genre and sub-genre sell well. It is essential to know what it is you are trying to achieve with your book. And you need to figure this out before you start trying to find a home for your work.

Before I move on, I'd like to address a common question: 'If I've already self-published, is it too late to go down a traditional market route with that book or with another one?'

The answer is: 'No, but…'

Think back to the section about agents and what they are looking for. Agents want to 'discover' a book that editors are going to get into a bidding war over. Editors are looking for a book that they can launch with a buzz into the market.

If you self-publish a book and it has minimal sales or poor reviews, you will struggle to find any agent willing to consider that title. Even if you remove the title from circulation completely before querying, the internet has a long memory. Commissioning editors don't want to launch an ad campaign shouting, 'Read this fantastic new book!' and have online reviewers complain, 'Hey, what are you trying to pull? I read that book two years ago!' If that happens, the editor will be going back to the agent with a rather cross email. So, generally speaking, logic states that submissions for books that have already been self-published struggle to get out of what agents call the 'slush pile'.

However, if you self-publish and the book sells well, you now have the publishing equivalent of Schrödinger's cat. Traditionally publishing your book is at once much more likely and much less desirable. Traditional publishers may be interested in leveraging your existing reader base or taking a popular title and exposing it to a wider audience. They will also be keen to secure a rising author and help them get physical books into bookstores. But if you are a successful self-publisher, do you really want to sacrifice a portion of your profits to a publisher if they will add little value?

If you have self-published a book but want to essentially 'try it again' through a more traditional route, smaller publishers and indie presses are your best bet as they tend to be more relaxed about this. They recognise that writers will sometimes self-publish a book so that their friends and family can enjoy it, without any plans to market it outside of their direct network. In this case, the first version isn't viewed as any sort of litmus test for the ultimate success of a traditionally published version down the line.

CHAPTER THREE

Picking Your Route to Market

Before we go any further, let's talk about genre.

Genre will be the first major factor in guiding your progress along the publishing pathway. Even if you are determined to go down the traditional pathway, you will need to know your book's genre before you begin. For example, there is no point sending your sci-fi erotica to an agent who says on their website that they are looking for literary fiction. Conversely, if you have a very beautifully written work of literary fiction or poetry, it's going to be a tough sell on an e-retailer's platform that is great at selling sci-fi erotica. You are likely better off trying to find a niche publisher that falls in love with your prose style and wants to champion it, not only bringing it to market but also sending it off to the right prizes where it might get the recognition it deserves.

It can be a problem if your book straddles more than one genre. Let's say you've written a novel about aliens that land in World War II and create havoc. Is your book sci-fi or historical fiction? If it has aliens, it's sci-fi. What if it is about a couple that meet and fall in love but are tragically separated during World War II – is this romance or historical fiction?

This is the problem with cross-genre books. Single-genre books are much easier to market. Traditional publishers look for books that fit neatly into their imprints (brands – see Chapter Five) and will immediately appeal to their readers. They won't take the time to explain to the world why this cross-genre work has some appealing aspects. They'd rather market a book which is immediately identifiable with their chosen genre. The same is true with self-publishing. When you upload your book onto the online retailer's platform, the first thing they will want you to do is to select the category. While it is not impossible to choose more than one, you are better off using those category options to target sub-genres than competing master categories.

Some genres have hard-and-fast rules about content and cover art. Writers who fail to comply with the genre conventions confuse readers and get bad reviews. For example, many avid romance readers think that romance novels must end either with a 'happily ever after' or a 'happy for now'. If your book's ending is closer to that of *Romeo and Juliet*, you're better off marketing it as women's fiction. Equally, if you write a lovely little mystery set around an eighty-year-old amateur sleuth, you wouldn't want to list it as a police procedural, even if it goes into detail on the police work.

One of the hardest books to categorise is one that straddles a specific genre and literary fiction. If you have written a really great genre classic, but used beautiful, stylised prose, you might be wondering why you can't place it. The literary writing style may be the reason. This isn't to say that you need to rewrite the book to move it into one category, as this would make for a boring world. However, it helps to be aware of this challenge.

What exactly is literary fiction? This is one of the hardest genre definitions for writers to understand. There are a number of different definitions for what literary fiction is, but generally, a literary fiction book would be likely to have a very high quality of writing and cover something 'important', whether that is a political situation, an issue of human feeling or emotion, or a period of history. If it is a historical work, it's likely to be intensely researched, so that every bit of the world and the politics of the time is as accurate as it can be. Literary fiction can be complex and more challenging to read, such as Anna Burns' Booker Prize-winning *Milkman* – this complexity can attract criticism of the genre. Conversely, there is no doubt that Hemingway would be considered literary because of his skill and originality in writing and the subjects he covers, but he is famous for his simple sentence structures.

*

Before we turn to a discussion of which path is best for your book, I recommend you take a few minutes to fill in the following three questionnaires. There aren't any right or wrong answers, but they are intended to crystallise what it is you want to achieve for your book, for yourself as an author and for your writing career. Once you've completed the questionnaires, keep the answers in mind when you turn to the next section, which outlines which routes to market work well for which sorts of books, writing and goals.

Quiz 1: Your book

Tick which of the following your book might best fit into. You can tick more than one box if absolutely necessary, but try to go for just one:

<u>Non-fiction</u>

- ❑ Biography/memoir
- ❑ Business
- ❑ Cookery
- ❑ Crafts, hobbies and home
- ❑ Criticism and scholarly research
- ❑ Health and fitness
- ❑ History, politics and social sciences
- ❑ Informational/instructional
- ❑ Narrative non-fiction
- ❑ Parenting
- ❑ Personal development
- ❑ Popular science
- ❑ Religion and spirituality
- ❑ Travel

Fiction

- ❑ Children's books
- ❑ Comics and graphic novels
- ❑ Commercial women's fiction
- ❑ Crime, thrillers and mystery
- ❑ Historical fiction
- ❑ Horror
- ❑ Humour
- ❑ Literary fiction
- ❑ Romance
- ❑ Science fiction and fantasy
- ❑ Young adult

Other

- ❑ Drama
- ❑ Poetry

Quiz 2: Your intentions

Tick each of the following that you feel matches your intentions:

- ❏ I want to be a famous writer
- ❏ I want to get recognition from my peers for my thoughts
- ❏ I want to be on the bestseller lists
- ❏ I want to win literary prizes
- ❏ I want to be a household name
- ❏ I want to be on TV
- ❏ I just want to have a beautiful book in my hands which I can give to friends and family
- ❏ I want to walk into a bookstore and see my book on the shelf
- ❏ I want to stand outside a bookstore and see my book in the window
- ❏ I want to have a book launch party with my friends and family in my local bookstore

- ❑ I have a message which I want to reach as many people as possible
- ❑ I have a message which I want to be available to a certain community of people

Quiz 3: Your career goals

In a few sentences, if a commentator were to look back, in five years' time, at your writing career, what would you wish for them to say?

_____

_____

_____

_____

_____

_____

_____

_____

_____

_____

CHAPTER FOUR

Preparing to Start Your Journey to Publication

In a Facebook writer's group, someone recently asked, 'I've written my first chapter and outlined the rest of my book. When can I start looking for an agent?'

The excitement of having a book idea, writing the first chapter or finally getting to 'The End' on your first draft can be hard to manage. However, one of the biggest mistakes debut and emerging authors make is to try to bring a book to market too early. Before you take another step towards publishing, let's take a moment to discuss the bare minimum work you should do first.

Fiction

You cannot do anything with a fiction book until you have a completed manuscript. This can be confusing to new writers who are busily looking at agent and publisher submission requirements that request a synopsis and no more than the first three chapters. It is not uncommon for writers to see this and assume that having made an outline and a start is sufficient to get the publishing ball rolling. Let me be clear: it is not. The query letter, synopsis and sample chapters are the first hurdle. If an agent or publisher likes what they see, they will request the full manuscript, with the expectation that you will send it promptly. You won't have time to write and edit a manuscript at this point, and delays may mean your potential agent or publisher loses interest. Worse, they may become frustrated and feel that you have wasted their time.

If you are a debut or emerging fiction author, you will have to buckle down and write a complete book before you get any sort of advance or commitment to publishing. This is why you so often hear of writers who write early in the morning, late at night and over their lunch hour, finding time while holding down a regular job.

What happens when you complete your first draft? Is it okay to start querying? In all honesty, no. Most first drafts are terrible, particularly if you are a new writer, but sometimes even if you are a well-established one. Write your first draft, stick it in a drawer for at least a month, then go through it and edit. It can be tempting to jump straight to edits, but wait as long as you can. This delay allows you to approach the editing process with a fresh set of eyes.

Once you've edited your first draft, you still aren't ready to send it to an agent or publisher. Both of these groups of individuals will tell you to submit your best possible draft, and few of us are capable of fairly reviewing our own work. You need beta readers. Beta readers can be friends or strangers, fans of the genre or fellow writers. The most important criteria is their ability to be thoughtful and honest in their critique. Ask them to share their thoughts on your storyline, your characters and your setting – in other words, the big-picture elements. Try to get at least three to four viewpoints, so that you don't get stuck weighing up a 'he said, she said' situation.

With your beta readers' feedback in hand, do another edit of your book, addressing any concerns or issues that they raised. If you are struggling to make sense of feedback or are unsure how best to go about addressing it, you may want to consider hiring a developmental editor. I will provide more information on editors in Chapter Six.

Regardless of whether you are writing flash fiction, short stories, novelettes, novellas or books, putting together a well-crafted story takes time. Rushing through the process, particularly on your first few books, will not benefit you. You can use tools such as Grammarly and ProWritingAid to help guide your editing process, but don't depend on them to do everything for you.

Non-fiction

Non-fiction is somewhat different in that you do not need to have a completed manuscript before beginning the querying process. If you are interested in writing a non-fiction book such as a memoir, biography or educational text, you will need to build up a book proposal and write at least one sample chapter.

Preparing a book proposal is far from a quick and simple task. Most book proposals range from ten to twenty-five pages, providing a business case to potential agents and publishers for why your non-fiction book is marketable.

The marketability of your book will revolve around either your own marketability (for a memoir or autobiography), that of the person who is your main subject (for a biography) or the topicality of your subject matter (for an instructional or educational text). You will need to do research into the specific market for your work, ideally providing examples of similar titles that have performed well to show that there is a market for your book. Next you must explain how your book provides a new perspective compared to similar titles. For example, does your book explore a unique angle or feature exclusive content? Make sure to include this in your pitch.

Your proposal should include an outline of the content you intend to cover, references to any external experts you may consult and your author bio. It must also include sample chapters – at least one – written to the highest possible standard. Do NOT submit a rushed first draft.

The final piece of a non-fiction proposal is your marketing plan. Who is your target audience, why will they be interested in your book and how are you going to reach them? This is not a section for you to outline what you expect a publisher to deliver. This is about you, your platform and your reach. Your plans need to be clear, concrete and well thought out.

While fiction writers are locked away writing draft after draft, non-fiction writers would be better off focusing on getting writing credits in relevant newspapers, magazines, journals and websites. The more impressive a list you can build before you start the querying process, the better placed you are to have a chance at success. You should also try to gain a following on one or more social channels and begin building up a list of email subscribers. If you do not have some form of writing credentials and an audience of followers, you are very probably not getting a book deal.

If you are a debut author writing a narrative-driven memoir and you do not have a platform, you should prepare to submit a complete draft rather than a sample chapter. If you can demonstrate your writing abilities and tell a compelling story while showing that this story is marketable, you might be able to overcome the requirement for a platform.

CHAPTER FIVE

Traditional Publishing

If you've determined that traditional publishing is the right place for you and your book, and you've edited your manuscript into the best possible shape, you are now ready to enter the querying process.

Before you start emailing out submissions, you will need to do some groundwork.

Step 1: Query materials

Fiction

Although agent and publisher submission guidelines will vary, you can save yourself some time by preparing the basic common elements: a query letter, a brief synopsis and various manuscript excerpts (first five pages, first chapter, first three chapters, etc.).

Your query letter should be short, precise and factual. It should include a strong 'hook' designed to excite and intrigue agents; information on the genre, word count and comparable titles; and a small bio about yourself. It doesn't need to explain how your book ends. It almost goes without saying that your writing in the query letter must rank among your best work. Don't treat a query letter like a traditional cover letter you'd send with a CV. Do research examples and guidance online: many agents have blogged on this topic. Do share your query letter with other writers for feedback. If you are struggling, you may want to invest in query writing services.

Synopsis requests range from one page max to three to five pages. A synopsis should broadly outline your story. It must include the ending. Do include information on all of your story arcs. Don't list the name of every character. Agents and publishers want to see that you know how to structure a story – you need to include as much information as needed to illustrate this point, but equally no more than necessary.

Non-fiction
Similarly to fiction submissions, non-fiction writers will need to prepare a query letter and at least one sample chapter. They will also need a well-written book proposal.

Your book proposal is key to selling a non-fiction work, and should be viewed more as a business plan than a synopsis. The proposal should include the following information: an analysis of comparable titles (ideally recent ones); an overview of the demographics of the target audience; a detailed marketing plan; your bio (explaining why you are the right person to write this book); and a chapter outline or table of contents.

One of the most critical components of a non-fiction pitch is the author bio. You must demonstrate that you have the required expertise and that you have an audience of followers. This is particularly true in the highly competitive categories of memoir, health, business and self-help.

Step 2: Choosing agents and publishers to query

There are more than 1000 literary agencies in the United States, and no small number in the UK. Small publishers and indie presses also abound. They vary in size, scope, interests and experience. Under no circumstances would it make sense to query all of them. How then do you narrow them down and create a target list? Here are a few ideas for where you might start:

- Comparable titles and authors: Find out who represents them and who publishes them, and see if those agencies and publishers are accepting submissions within your genre.

- Trade associations: Many writers' associations allow agents and publishers to have affiliate memberships, or they may publish a list of relevant agents. Often this information is only accessible to members, so you may need to ask another writer to help if you can't access it.

- Manuscript Wish List, Publishers Marketplace, Agent Query, Query Tracker and Jericho Writers, among others, all publish searchable directories of both agents and small publishers. You can use their tools not only to identify potential places to pitch, but also to find information on submission criteria and latest interests.

- If you prefer paper format, you may want to check out the annual editions of the *Writers' & Artists' Yearbook* (UK) or the *Writer's Market* series (US). These books provide contact information for literary agents and publishers, as well as other organisations, with a broad lens on what it means to be published. If you are looking for media outlets where you can pitch content to gain credentials for a non-fiction proposal, this could be particularly helpful. They offer more tools and indexes online at an additional cost.

- Agent location: You can shop your manuscript around to agents outside of your own country, particularly if your book (or you) has an obvious connection with another part of the world. When looking into agents abroad, you still need to identify those who are most likely to be interested in your genre and you should consider where they focus their efforts. Signing with an agent in one country does not limit your opportunities to sell publishing rights abroad. Agents and publishers alike often have foreign rights desks which negotiate publishing agreements with other countries. Given the challenge of signing with one agent, you may be better off allowing your existing agent or publisher to negotiate selling the foreign rights rather than starting the whole pitching process again.

Step 3: Submitting

Now that you have prepared your query materials and have a list of agents and publishers to pitch, you are ready to begin the submission process. Here are some tips to keep in mind as you go:

- Read their submission guidelines! Be sure you know why you are sending your writing to them and that what you send is what they are looking for. Send them exactly the materials they request, no less and no more. Make sure you send materials in the requested format – some people won't accept attachments.

- Submit your queries using their preferred contact channel. If you meet an agent at an event and they give you permission to email them, go for it. However, if an agent states that they will only accept queries submitted in a particular way (to a specific email address, with a specific subject line or via an online form), use that channel. Do not try to be clever and send unrequested materials through an alternative channel. Most agent and publisher websites provide explicit instructions for submitting queries – start there if you are unsure.

- Do not query your entire list in one go. You have one chance to query an agency or publisher. Start small, choosing a mix of your dream agents and some who are less interesting. Wait for feedback, adjusting your query letter or synopsis as needed before sending out the next round of submissions.

- You are a professional writer sending a manuscript, not a marketing agent sending a book. Don't use overly sales-y language.

- No mocked-up covers, strange formatting of the pages or password-protected documents.

- Explain (succinctly) why you are sending them a query, showing that you have done your homework. Don't say that you are querying other agents – they know this already.

- Don't lie or stretch the truth.

- Don't pay a 'reading fee' to any agent. Reputable agents and publishers do not charge fees for submissions.

- Avoid 'Dear Sirs'! The majority of staff at agencies and publishers are female. Try gender-neutral options instead, such as 'Dear ABC Agency' or 'Dear Agency team' if you are not addressing your submission to a specific individual.

- Feel free to engage with agents and publishers on Twitter, but DO NOT pitch them your book on Twitter or in a LinkedIn message. Follow the instructions on their websites and submit through the proper channels. Agents and publishers receive a large number of queries and often have tracking systems or methods in place to manage them. Social media messages are difficult to track; if you use them to submit your work, your query is more likely to be ignored or lost.

- Use Twitter events such as #PitMad to test out your hook and see if any agents or publishers bite.

Step 4: Waiting and follow-up

Once you have begun querying agents and publishers, you should be prepared for a lengthy waiting game. Now is the time to develop a thick skin. Everyone receives rejections. Even famous writers have a pile of them. James Patterson, one of the highest-earning authors of the last few years, received thirty-one rejections on the first book in his *Alex Cross* series. Dr Seuss, a household name around the world, was rejected twenty-seven times before an editor friend agreed to take a look at his first book. Rejections are so common that J. K. Rowling famously shared a selection of her rejection letters on Twitter to inspire other writers to keep going.

Most rejections are form letters, and should not be taken as any statement on your work. In some cases, agents may provide helpful advice or insight into why your work isn't a fit for them at this time. Agents and publishers have also been known to propose that an author revise and resubmit their manuscript, providing specific guidance on which aspects of the work should be changed. Although it can be disheartening to be told you need to make more edits or rewrites, you should view a 'revise and resubmit' response as positive feedback.

However, there is no guarantee that the agent or publisher will offer a contract once you have made the edits, particularly if you take a long time to do so. The market may move on, their list may become full or they may still feel that the book isn't right for them. You should take their advice to heart, but remain open-minded about further queries.

Once a query is submitted, it can end up in one of three places: the slush pile, a reader's inbox or the agent's inbox. The slush pile is the industry term for unsolicited manuscripts, referring back to the days when authors posted physical copies of their manuscript to agents and publishers, which would pile up on a desk. Larger agencies and publishers who receive high numbers of submissions will put manuscripts into electronic versions of the slush pile, where they will be reviewed as and when someone has time to look at them. This task might be assigned to interns or other junior staffers.

Some agents hire readers to help them manage their submissions. Readers will review queries and prepare a report, either recommending rejection or flagging up potential good fits to the main agent for further consideration. In some cases, junior agents act as readers for more experienced agents, learning the business under the guidance of a mentor.

Lastly, there are the agents who personally read all submissions. However, there is no guarantee they will read beyond the first few lines of your query letter, so make sure you capture their interest straight away.

Your goal is to find an agent or publisher who loves your book as much as you do. Love, as we know, is subjective. You may have the most fantastically written book of all time, but if an agent cannot get into the story, they will still pass.

If an agent is interested in your work, they will request your manuscript in full. This is why you want to have a polished manuscript ready before you begin querying. There are horror stories about writers who got an immediate request for a full manuscript and had to rush out a draft in the span of several hours.

After a full read, an agent may present you with an offer of representation. You do not have to accept this on the spot. In fact, you should not. If you get an offer, you should update any other agent who is still in the process of reviewing your submission. The fact that one agent loves your book will often encourage them to move you to the top of their reading pile. In an ideal world, you will get another offer and you can make an informed decision about which agent is the best one to represent your work to publishers.

Step 5: Finding a publisher

If you have contracted with an agent and not directly with a small publisher, your agent will now begin pitching your book to commissioning editors within publishing houses. They will pitch to both large and small publishers, depending on your genre. Landing an agent is in no way a guarantee that you will a) sell your book to a publisher or b) sell your book to a 'big five' publisher.

The agent works on your behalf, providing advice and guidance throughout the remainder of the process. They will start with a review of your work, potentially suggesting further edits. Once they are happy with your manuscript, they will submit it to commissioning editors at a small selection of publishers for consideration. Their goal is to attract as many interested parties as possible, with the aim of getting the best deal for you as the author. Once you have an offer from a publisher, your agent will work on your behalf to negotiate the contract. They will weigh up advances, rights and marketing support, negotiating each of these with the publisher based on your preferences. For example, an author with a strong reader following may want a bigger advance and more control over their book marketing, in exchange for reduced marketing support from the publisher after the launch date. A debut author without much of a following may prefer the reverse. Your agent can negotiate publishing rights across formats (e-book, print, audio), by country (single territory, multi-territory or worldwide) and by length of time.

Before moving on to the next step, let's speak briefly about imprints. Many publishing houses, both large and small, will distribute books under various brand names. These brand names are known as imprints. For example, Jonathan Cape is an imprint of Vintage, which is itself an imprint of Penguin Random House, the largest UK publishing group. Some imprints formerly existed as independent publishers in their own right and at some point were bought up by larger publishers – Virago Books is one example, having started life as an indie press in the 1970s and now continuing as an imprint of Hachette. For the average reader, the imprint, or indeed the publisher, is irrelevant. Imprints become relevant when it comes to booksellers, prize authorities and sometimes the media. Large publishers use imprints to divide up the vast array of books they publish each year into an understandable order and will have different departments or even subsidiary companies to manage them. Each imprint will usually have its own specialism – for example, mystery novels, contemporary romance, classics or literary fiction. Booksellers can more quickly understand where these books should be promoted and shelved, aiding them in their consideration of whether to stock them.

The average layperson cannot tell the difference between an imprint and a small press, and this can cause consternation for writers who have signed with an imprint but want to crow about their association with the larger publishing house. Work closely with your agent to understand each imprint's reputation and connections before agreeing to sign with one as your publisher.

Step 6: Congrats, you've sold your book!

Signing a contract with a publisher, either large or small, is cause for celebration. As you can see, it is far from an easy task. However, be prepared to get back to work the next day. Your commissioning editor will undoubtedly require more rounds of editing, your publisher will want to discuss marketing plans and you will need to step up your efforts to build an audience of interested readers. The more work you personally put into promoting your book, the higher the chances of your success.

Final thoughts

You will note that I have not spoken about cover design, layout or distribution. This is because these items are all handled by your publisher, often with little or no input from yourself. The only exception is if you are working with a hybrid publisher. If you make it past the hybrid publisher's submission process and they offer you a contract, you will be more involved in the selection of the editor, the creation of the cover art and setting timelines. You are given this right because you are helping to pay for these elements. However, this involvement may come with limits. For example, your contract could include three cover images for consideration – but not an unlimited amount. Your hybrid publisher will guide you on genre conventions for both style and cover art – you would do well to listen to them.

You might also note that I have not outlined any timelines for finding an agent or a publisher, or for the publication process. Quite simply, there is no rule of thumb. It might all happen within ten months. It could also take ten years. Really.

CHAPTER SIX

Self-publishing

If you've assessed the traditional publishing options and feel that none of them is right for you, the alternative route is to self-publish. Before we get into the details of how you would self-publish a book, let's first explore the reasons why you might be publishing.

Reason 1: For friends and family

For some writers, simply being able to hand printed copies of your book to friends and family may be enough. In this case, you may choose to forgo expensive editing, cover design services and ISBN purchases, and go direct to any one of the book printing services you can find online.

Reason 2: For wider distribution

If you intend to sell your book to readers outside of your friends and family and make money doing so, congratulations. You're not just self-publishing, you're starting a publishing business. Let's focus on the business of publishing a book, setting aside the topic of income expectations until the next chapter.

Step 1: Hiring editors

Now that you are running a mini publishing company, hiring an editor is no longer optional. It is not possible to fully edit your own work – your brain begins to fill in gaps and auto-correct errors, making it impossible for you to catch every error and typo on your own. You should budget in the cost of securing external support.

There is plenty of discussion about the number of different types of editors. I am going to break them into three categories, for simplicity's sake.

- Developmental editors: These editors review your storyline, world-building, character development and tone of voice. A good developmental editor will provide you with a broad overview of your work using the above categories, as well as making more detailed edits within your manuscript. A developmental editor does not do copy-edits. Developmental editors are an invaluable resource for unpicking tricky beta reader feedback to address issues of pacing, or for helping you to understand where there are gaps between what you know as the writer and what the reader can see.

- Copy-editors: These editors check your manuscript on a line-by-line basis, identifying and correcting misspellings, typos and grammatical mistakes. They may also provide suggestions for rephrasing – either within paragraphs or for larger chunks of writing. In addition, they will check there are no inconsistencies in the book or flaws in the timeline. Once you feel you have a final draft, you are ready to hire a copy-editor.

- Proofreaders: These professionals are your final line of defence against the dreaded typo. Proofreaders take the proverbial magnifying glass to your most final of final drafts or to the typeset proofs of your book, correcting any tiny spelling errors or misplaced punctuation that have slipped through the net earlier in the process. Proofreaders may guarantee a certain percentage of accuracy, but be wary of anyone who promises a 100% guarantee. Even traditionally published bestsellers can still have a typo slip through.

A common question in self-publishing groups is when to hire an editor. From an expense point of view, you should wait until you have done as much as you can yourself. Developmental editors and copy-editors often charge by the hour, so the cleaner your draft, the faster they can be. Editors may request that you send a representative sample of your manuscript, such as a chapter or five to ten pages. They review the sample to assess the work required and use that to prepare an estimate for you. You do not have to send them the first chapter or first few pages of your manuscript, and may instead want to send a sample that best represents how thorough a review is required.

If you have a limited budget for editorial support, I recommend you find a good writing partner and a dependable group of beta readers. They can act as free developmental editors, helping you shape your story and your prose without requiring payment.

How do you pick the right editor for your book? Ideally, you would prepare a shortlist of editors who have experience with your genre. This is where networking comes in handy – writers are always happy to share information on editors, both good and bad. Sometimes it can be more valuable to know which editors have a habit of disappearing halfway through a project than it is to know who is great to work with.

Editors' schedules can be booked out months in advance, so do not wait until the last minute to start looking for one. Contact your shortlist as early as you can, providing each of them with a few pages for a sample edit. Many professional editors will happily provide you with a sample edit at a low cost or free of charge. Assess the sample edits to see which editor is right for your project. Don't assume that the most expensive is necessarily the best!

You should also consider the editor's qualifications. Do they have professional training or a degree or qualification related to language, editing or writing? Are they a member of a professional society or other recognised group of copy-editors or proofreaders? You may also want to consider their ability to edit to particular standards and styles, such as US versus UK English.

Step 2: Cover designs

I asked a number of self-published authors where they invest their budgets, and the answers were nearly always the same: editors and cover designers. Your cover design can make or break your success. It is the first thing prospective readers see, and a low-quality cover will turn them away in an instant.

Before you think about your own cover design, start by researching similar titles in your genre. Sort by bestselling books to see which covers are attracting readers. It may be helpful to create a wish list on an e-tailer platform, saving all of the covers that catch your eye. Study them to understand genre constraints and where you may have room to play around.

Once you have an idea of which types of covers you like, you can begin your search for a cover designer. There are two options – pre-made and bespoke. Many professional cover designers offer pre-made covers at affordable prices. You can simply add your title and name and you are ready to go. Others may allow for minimal personalisation, such as changing the background colour.

If you have something more unique in mind, you can choose to have a bespoke cover designed. Again, you should work with a designer who has experience in your genre. Make sure they understand genre conventions so that you don't end up too far outside of the norm. Bespoke covers can vary wildly in price, so be clear upfront about your budget constraints.

If you are planning a series, you may want to buy more than one cover at a time, to ensure you can get a consistent look across all of the books.

Step 3: Layout and formatting

Your book is edited, you've got a cover – what next? Layout and formatting are now at the top of your list. Before you begin, you need to decide how you will distribute your book. Will you start with digital only? Would you also like to make a printed copy? Is paperback enough, or do you need hardback or large-print editions as well? All of these decisions will inform how you proceed with layout and formatting.

Once you have determined which layouts you need, you will have several options to choose from in order to produce them. Before you start any formatting work, consult with your planned retailers and printers to gather their guidelines. Follow them exactly. This is likely to mean you will need to prepare multiple different final files. For example, you would need a different file for regular type versus large print and for a small paperback versus a large hardback, and even different formats for the individual e-book retailers. Here are some examples of tools commonly used to format manuscripts for publication:

- Microsoft Word: If you have a simple, text-only book which you plan to digitally publish, Microsoft Word might be sufficient for your needs.

- Book writing software: Software specifically designed for authors, such as Scrivener, may include compiling capability, allowing you to output your book in formats for electronic and print publishing.

- Vellum and Draft2Digital: Serious self-publishing authors swear by these automated layout and formatting tools. They are particularly useful if you want to add in custom graphics, fancy type or stylised back matter.

- InDesign: If you have professional design skills and a lot of time, you can also use InDesign to format your book. It is preferred by writers who want total control over font, kerning (the spacing between letters in a printed book) and other typesetting features.

Step 4: ISBN/ASIN

Before you can distribute your book, you will need an internationally recognised book registration number. These come in two formats: International Standard Book Number (ISBN) and Amazon Standard Identification Number (ASIN). An ISBN is universally recognised, whereas an ASIN can only be used on Amazon.

The ISBN is used by booksellers, libraries, online retailers and anyone within the supply chain to identify the publisher, title, edition and format. You have two options for getting an ISBN for your book:

- Purchase a block of ISBNs: If you are planning to self-publish on more than one platform and/or more than one book, you may want to invest in a block of ISBNs. You will need one ISBN for each format of your book (i.e. one for e-book, one for paperback, one for hardback, etc.). The ISBN tells retailers about the publisher, title and format. You can buy single numbers or blocks of ten, a hundred or more. ISBNs are distributed in each country by the authorised reseller (such as Bowker in the US and Nielsen in the UK).

- Use an ISBN/ASIN provided by your distributor: Some distributors, such as Ingram and Amazon, will provide you with a registration number free of charge. You can only use that registration number on their platform, and it will list them as the publisher of your book in official records.

When you register your book's ISBN number(s), you can specify additional metadata related to the title, such as genre and keywords. Make sure this information is complete and accurate, as retailers and libraries will use this to find and promote the book. If a retailer or library is looking for books on a specific topic, you do not want to miss out on the chance of distribution simply because you failed to put in the correct metadata.

Step 5: Printing and distributing

Before you send your book off for a sizeable print run, you will want to print a small batch of proof copies. Proof copies allow you to make sure that your cover and interior are printing as you expected, and to correct any issues before you begin distributing them. How many proof copies you order is up to you, but it can be helpful to order extras if you need to send hard copies to any advance reviewers.

You have two options for large-scale printing of your book: offset printing or print-on-demand. Offset printing is when you commission a specific printing house to produce a quantity of your books in advance. Publishers typically commission an offset print run of books they plan to distribute to bookstores, gathering orders in advance. If you print more than you can immediately distribute, you will need to plan for storage and shipping of the remaining copies. For this reason, offset printing is not common for self-published books.

Most self-published authors opt for a print-on-demand service. In this case, you upload your layout files to the printing platform and they print a copy whenever one is ordered. You do not need to print a minimum quantity in advance and there is no stock to store. The advantage of print-on-demand is that your book is never out of stock as it can be printed any time anyone orders. The downside is that buyers may experience a longer lead time when placing an order as the book must be printed before it can be shipped.

If you are planning to pitch your book to brick-and-mortar bookstores, you must take distribution into account when selecting your printer. Some popular e-tailers offer printing options for authors, but do not offer viable distribution to bookstores. Independent booksellers will certainly frown if you approach them about stocking an e-tailer-printed book. If you use a print-on-demand service, you should double-check how they offer distribution. Many smaller print-on-demand services partner with international distributors such as Ingram, acting as a middleman between you and the actual distributor.

If bookstores are an important part of your distribution plan, you should think about stock and returns. Bookstores will want the ability to return unsold copies of a book, particularly if the author is not well-known. You may be better off printing a small number and talking with local bookstores about consignment selling. In consignment selling, you provide the bookstore with an agreed number of physical copies of your book. The bookstore will sell these on your behalf, and will either pay you a set price per book or a share of the margin. At the end of the consignment period, the bookstore will return any unsold copies to you. This allows them to offer your book without taking on the risk of unsold copies. You may want to try this with select bookstores to gather sales information, which you can use in discussions with other bookstores.

CHAPTER SEVEN

Income Expectations

According to a 2005 survey by the Authors' Licensing and Collecting Society (ALCS), 40% of the respondents stated that their income came entirely from writing. The same survey, run in 2017 with the results published in 2018, found that only 13.7% of authors were living entirely off their writing careers.[1]

Over the past fifteen years, authors' pay has shifted dramatically from a reasonable median to a drastic level of inequality between the bestselling superstars and everyone else. According to a 2019 report from the ALCS, 'There is considerable inequality of earning power amongst authors, with the highest-earning 10% of writers taking home about 70% of total earnings in the profession.'[2]

---

[1] Kretschmer, Martin et al. *UK Authors' Earnings and Contracts 2018: A Survey of 50,000 Writers*. UK Copyright and Creative Economy Centre, University of Glasgow (independent research commissioned by Authors' Licensing and Collecting Society), 2018. Available at: <https://wp.alcs.co.uk/app/uploads/2018/06/ALCS-Authors-earnings-2018.pdf>

[2] Society of Authors. 'Report on authors' earnings has worrying implications for diversity'. 7 May 2019. Available at: <https://www.societyofauthors.org/News/News/2019/May/Report-on-authors-earnings-diversity-implications>

What can you expect to earn by publishing your book? In all likelihood, not a huge amount. If you work hard, write well and market your book effectively, you may earn something. Earning anything sizeable, however, is a significant challenge.

The publishing industry

To understand today's publishing marketplace, you need to view it through the lens of the reader. The reality of the self-publishing and digital-first phenomena is that there are many more books available than there used to be, spanning a vast range of quality. In this modern era, when we are presented with a mind-boggling array of books to choose from online (Amazon alone has over forty-four million items in the Books category), it's often argued that the way a consumer makes a choice is by following the herd. Choosing a book at the top of the bestseller charts is a safe way to ensure the book isn't poorly written drivel (though 'quality' might be a matter for discussion in this regard) and it's also the easiest search mechanism.

Once the reader has made a purchase, the algorithms take over, suggesting similar titles and tracking whether the reader clicks through to learn more.

This means that books at the top of the charts sell and stay at the top of the charts. Similar books find it easy to ride their coat-tails. This is why it is worthwhile for publishing houses to invest all their funds in a few choice books – getting them to the top of the charts in one quick boost and then letting the nature of search algorithms do the rest of the heavy lifting.

If you are self-publishing, this is also going to be your aim – but it's no easy matter.

This exact same phenomenon is also prevalent in the music industry. In his book *Move Fast and Break Things*, Jonathan Taplin describes how 80% of revenue is now generated by 1% of the content, compared to the 1980s when 80% of revenue came from 20% of the content.[3]

Author income and the dying midlist

Twenty years ago, traditionally published authors gladly wore the badge of being 'midlist', releasing a steady stream of high-quality books without the pressure of having to hit the top of the charts. Shown visually, author earnings existed in a pyramidal structure, where a few books would earn big

[3]Taplin, Jonathan. *Move Fast and Break Things*. London: Macmillan, 2017.

bucks, a 'midlist' of authors would sell a good number of books and make something close to a living, and another big chunk of authors would not sell so well.

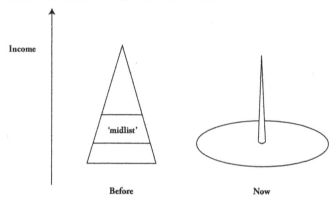

Figure Three: Author income

Today, author income looks dramatically different. We live in a world where most books sell just a few copies, but a few books sell in huge numbers. The vast majority of published authors, regardless of which publishing route they have chosen to reach their readership, live in the bottom pool rather than the spike (as shown in Figure Three).

What does this mean for which path you choose? It makes it all the more important to understand what it is you want to achieve from your writing.

Niche sellers

If you want your beautifully crafted collection of poetry to find its way into the hands of readers who will appreciate it, be realistic about the fact that it is very unlikely to sell in airport bookstores. You will probably not be able to make a living from this book. Your best bet would be to find a small publishing house or literary imprint that will be passionate about your writing. They can help you reach your target audience, as well as putting you forward for relevant prizes and awards. To fund your writing time, it could be worth your while to investigate grants and residencies.

Bestsellers

If you are really keen to be the next J. K. Rowling, Lee Child or Martina Cole, you need to write a book that stands a chance of sitting atop that spike. To do this, you need to be all over your genre, understanding it inside out, spotting trends early on and/or writing a book which agents and publishers are going to go wild for. Only then will they pay a big advance, justifying a big marketing spend to shoot it up the charts.

If you haven't written a bestseller but you do land a traditional publishing contract, you may be surprised by the size of your advance. If you are a debut author, your advance is likely to be in the range of £1,500–£5,000 (or around $2000–$6000), if you get one at all, and it won't be paid in one go. More likely, one third of your advance will be paid at contract signing, one third when the manuscript is delivered and the final third upon publication. You will need to sell a requisite number of copies of your book to earn out your advance, and only once this has been achieved will you see another royalty payment from your publisher. Unfortunately, the reality is that this will not be enough money to allow you to quit your day job.

The upside to traditional publishing is that you don't have to pay for editing or cover design and you don't have to deal with the hassle of formatting or distribution. The downside is that you will need to pay a commission to your agent (including out of your advance) and you cede the final decision-making for a lot of aspects of your finished book.

Making money from self-publishing

Craig Martelle and Michael Anderle sit among the top echelons of self-publishing success stories. They offer mentoring and guidance for other self-published authors through their Facebook group 20BooksTo50K. The idea behind the name is simple: to earn $50,000 per year as a self-published author, you need to write and publish twenty books. Then you need to sell enough copies of each of those books to earn $7.50 per book per day. It is a target that somehow manages to seem both accessible and completely out of reach at the same time.

If you spend any time in their group, or follow along with other similar guides, you'll quickly see that successful self-published authors focus on rapid-release, on-trend series, with schedules ranging from four to twelve books per year. The idea is to game the e-tailer algorithms, keeping sales high and avoiding the ninety-day death drop when most book marketing runs out of steam. Box sets, anthologies and novellas help to fill in the gaps.

You have to find the upfront investment, and in return you get to keep a larger percentage of the profits. However, a larger percentage of zero or some other small number isn't going to balance out the investment required to publish a high-quality book. I have yet to find anyone who is willing to suggest taking out a business loan to cover the investment costs – the market is viewed as far too risky and uncertain by all of the authors I know.

That said, it is possible to make money as a self-published author. Nearly every day, self-published authors post their success stories in Facebook groups like 20BooksTo50K, sharing their journey from being a debut author to earning a sustainable income from their books. While there are some lucky individuals whose first book skyrockets them to success, most self-published success stories are the product of hard work, great writing and clever marketing. There are more of these longer-term success stories than many people would imagine, as these authors are typically not included in industry surveys.

CHAPTER EIGHT

A Word on Marketing

When you finally hold your book in your hands, or see it for sale on a digital platform, it feels like you can release the breath you've been holding for weeks and months on end.

I am here to tell you that you still have more work to do. If you want your book to sell and to reach your target audience, you must be willing to market it.

It isn't just self-published authors who are worried about marketing strategies. Nowadays, agents and publishers alike are also asking their traditionally published authors what they will be doing to promote their book. 'Nothing' is no longer an acceptable answer. The simple truth is that you are your own best marketing resource.

If you are at the start of your writing journey, now is an excellent time to take stock of your abilities and interests, thinking about which marketing activities will be easiest for you. Some of these tactics, like blogging, building a newsletter subscriber list and acquiring a social media following, take time. Waiting until your book is done before you start means you are already too late.

If you are finished writing and are ready to take the next step towards publishing, there is a lot you should be doing to give your book the best chance of success. This is particularly true if you are planning to self-publish. Your mini publishing company must include a promotional department. If that isn't you, you need to budget for someone to assist you.

You may be surprised at the number of marketing tactics writers use to promote their work. The traditional book tour usually comes top of mine, but that doesn't mean that it is the best tactic for you. You should consider a long list of options so you can determine which combination best suits you and your book, and build a plan accordingly.

Ideally, you will want to begin your marketing work three to six months before your first book is published. Here is a broad overview of a selection of marketing tactics writers use to create awareness and drive interest in their books:

- Author websites and social media accounts: These allow your readers to find out more about your work and about you as the author. They also allow readers to connect with you directly.

- Mailing lists and newsletters: Writers are now much more sophisticated at using these traditional marketing tools to promote their work. Newsletters can be sent up to multiple times per month, sharing information on new reviews, opportunities to meet the author, special discounts or book swag like T-shirts and bookmarks.

- Automated funnels: What happens when someone signs up for your email list? Now, more authors are creating automated email campaigns which drip-feed information on their books and freebies. These 'set-it-and-forget-it' campaigns ensure every email subscriber gets sent the same starter emails, promoting books and offering special bonus material only available through the newsletter.

- Personal appearances: Book tours aren't limited to bookstores any longer. Authors participate in festivals, give speeches at events and conferences, organise discussion panels and even visit book clubs, all in the hopes of meeting new readers.

- Social media: Running your own social media accounts is the tip of the iceberg. You can make bookstagrammers and booktubers part of your promotional plan, capitalise on hashtags to increase the visibility of your posts, organise cover reveals and more.

As you select tactics for your book marketing plan, don't feel pressured to take them all on yourself. Think carefully about which ones you will enjoy the most and which ones will deliver the most value. Keep your reader at the centre of your thoughts, focusing on how you can best connect with them and build up a long-term relationship so they will read everything you write.

I will leave you with this last piece of advice: write what you love. Publish in a way that will leave you fulfilled and help you achieve your goals.

THE END

Additional Resources

As you begin your publishing journey, here are some resources which you may find useful:

Information on literary agents and publishers

Writers' & Artists' Yearbook (UK):
https://www.writersandartists.co.uk/

Writer's Market series (US):
https://www.writersmarket.com/

Manuscript Wish List:
https://www.manuscriptwishlist.com/

Publishers Marketplace:
https://www.publishersmarketplace.com/

Query Tracker:
https://querytracker.net/

AgentQuery:
https://www.agentquery.com/

Jericho Writers AgentMatch:
https://jerichowriters.com/agentmatch/

Information on the traditional publishing industry

The Bookseller (UK):
https://www.thebookseller.com/

Publishers Weekly (US):
https://www.publishersweekly.com/

Information on self-publishing

Alliance of Independent Authors:
https://www.allianceindependentauthors.org/

Independent Book Publishers Association:
https://www.ibpa-online.org/

20Booksto50K Facebook group:
https://www.facebook.com/groups/20Booksto50k/

Self-publishing Formula courses and conferences:
https://selfpublishingformula.com/

Professional editing associations

Chartered Institute of Editing and Proofreading (UK):
https://www.ciep.uk/

ACES: The Society for Editing (US):
https://aceseditors.org/

The Editorial Freelancers Association (US):
https://www.the-efa.org/

Industry watchdogs

Writer Beware:
https://www.sfwa.org/other-resources/for-authors/writer-beware/

Self-publishing Services Watchdog:
https://selfpublishingadvice.org/self-publishing-services-watchdog/

LYNN MORRISON

How to Market Your Book

These days, regardless of whether a book is self-published or traditionally published, there will be an expectation on the author to take an active role in marketing their book. Based on a series of interviews with successful authors from both sides of the publishing divide and both sides of the pond, Lynn lays out in detail the marketing strategies that have worked for them, alongside an explanation of how book marketing works based on her own long-standing career as a senior marketing exec.

From developing social media tactics and arranging promotional events to handling press and trying to start viral campaigns, Lynn offers practical advice designed to help an author find a book marketing strategy that best works for them, based on their personal strengths and budget.

'Morrison turns the overwhelming task of marketing into bite-size tips and tutorials that anyone can implement.'
— Stephanie Jankowski, author of *Schooled*

LUCINDA FORD

How to Sleep

Introducing eight easy-to-use techniques for falling asleep, *How to Sleep: A Natural Method* is an indispensable companion for those who find it difficult to fall asleep and stay asleep.

When sleeplessness becomes a regular occurrence, it can set up a vicious cycle of fatigue, anxiety and sleepless nights. Finding ways to turn off the racing mind and negative thoughts or stress when going to sleep is an essential step, allowing you to break that vicious cycle and move towards a place of better well-being. The eight simple sleep techniques, along with their accompanying notes, are designed to calm the mind and allow sleep to come naturally. They are distilled from the best of thinking from the East and the West, including cognitive behavioural therapy, mindfulness and meditation, taking lessons from each of these methods on how best to quiet your mind and find a calm place from which to fall asleep.

'How to Sleep *gives valuable advice and tips to help with many of the leading causes of sleeplessness without people needing a PhD to understand it.'*
— Ian Stockbridge, MNCS (Accred),
MBABCP, MBACP